Events That Shaped America

The Transcontinental
Railroad

Sabrina Crewe and Michael V. Uschan

Gareth Stevens Publishing

A WORLD ALMANAC EDUCATION GROUP COMPANY

Please visit our web site at: www.garethstevens.com
For a free color catalog describing Gareth Stevens Publishing's list of high-quality
books and multimedia programs, call 1-800-542-2595 (USA) or 1-800-387-3178
(Canada). Gareth Stevens Publishing's fax: (414) 332-3567.

Library of Congress Cataloging-in-Publication Data available upon request from publisher.
Fax (414) 336-0157 for the attention of the Publishing Records Department.

ISBN 0-8368-3401-1

This North American edition first published in 2004 by
Gareth Stevens Publishing
A World Almanac Education Group Company
330 West Olive Street, Suite 100
Milwaukee, WI 53212 USA

This edition © 2004 by Gareth Stevens Publishing.

Produced by Discovery Books
Editor: Sabrina Crewe
Designer and page production: Sabine Beaupré
Photo researcher: Sabrina Crewe
Maps and diagrams: Stefan Chabluk
Gareth Stevens editorial direction: Jim Mezzanotte
Gareth Stevens art direction: Tammy Gruenewald

Photo credits: Iris and B. Gerald Cantor Center for Visual Arts, Stanford University,
gift of David Hewes: p. 20; Central Pacific Railroad Photographic History Museum
(CPRR.org): pp. 4, 13, 19; Corbis: cover, pp. 5, 8, 10, 17 (top), 18, 21, 26; North Wind
Picture Archives: pp. 6, 7, 9, 11 (both), 12, 14, 15, 16, 17 (bottom), 22, 23, 24, 27.

Printed in the United States of America

1 2 3 4 5 6 7 8 9 08 07 06 05 04

Contents

Introduction 4

Chapter 1: Planning a Railroad 6

Chapter 2: Building the Railroad 12

Chapter 3: The Joining of the Rails 20

Chapter 4: From Coast to Coast 22

Conclusion 26

Time Line 28

Things to Think About and Do 29

Glossary 30

Further Information 31

Index 32

Introduction

An Important Event

In the days before people had cars and before airplanes flew back and forth across the country, railroads were a very important form of transportation. Compared to traveling by horse or by foot, **train** journeys were fast and comfortable. So when a railroad was built from the eastern part of the United States to the western part, it was a very important event.

The railroad actually only crossed the western half of the continent, but it was called the **Transcontinental** Railroad because it allowed people and goods to travel from one side of the country to the other by linking with existing railroads. This opportunity brought a big change—people could make a lot of money selling their products all over the nation and overseas, and the United States became richer as a result.

This map was drawn in 1908 to show places of interest along the Transcontinental Railroad. By 1908, the route reached all the way to the Pacific coast at San Francisco. The Central Pacific had merged with the Southern Pacific and taken on its name.

A modern train travels the Transcontinental Railroad through a tunnel high up in the Sierra Nevada. (*Sierra* means "mountain range" in Spanish.)

The railroad also helped people in the East to reach and settle in parts of the country where white people had never lived before.

Thousands of Workers

For over six years, from 1863 to 1869, thousands of workers labored on the Transcontinental Railroad. It cost millions of dollars to build. The railroad went through vast expanses of inhospitable desert, across rivers and canyons, and over towering mountains. Sometimes it went right through mountains, too.

A Joint Project

The Transcontinental Railroad was a joint project. The Union Pacific built 1,086 miles (1,747 kilometers) of railroad track west from Omaha, Nebraska. The Central Pacific came 689 miles (1,109 km) east from Sacramento, California. On May 10, 1869, the two linked their lines at Promontory Summit in Utah.

Rushing and Roaring
"I see over my own continent the Pacific railroad surmounting every barrier,
I see continual trains of cars winding along the Platte carrying freight and passengers,
I hear the locomotives rushing and roaring, and the shrill steam-whistle,
I hear the echoes reverberate through the grandest scenery in the world, . . .
Tying the Eastern to the Western sea, the road between Europe and Asia."

Walt Whitman, from "Passage to India," a poem about the Transcontinental Railroad

Planning a Railroad

Crossing the continent to take supplies west, a group of travelers struggles against a snowstorm. The journey on horse-back or by wagon took several months.

Between East and West

In the 1850s, the nation's population centers in the East and West were separated by a vast area. Although white settlement had pushed westward from the East, the center of the continent had not yet been taken over by white people. The area was home to several Native American peoples.

Everyone Wants a Railroad

"The sunburned immigrant, walking with his wife and little ones beside his gaunt and weary oxen in mid-continent, the sea-sick traveler, the homesick bride whose wedding trip had included a passage of the 'Isthmus' [across Panama, Central America], the merchant whose stock needed replenishing, everyone prayed for a Pacific railroad."

Hubert Howe Bancroft, nineteenth-century historian

There were both the original inhabitants of the region and tribes that had come later because they had been pushed out of their homelands in the East.

Traveling West

Before the Transcontinental Railroad was built, the journey from the East to California in the West took months. Pioneers in wagons perished from illness or lack of water or food, in accidents, or in battles with Native people. An ocean voyage around Cape Horn in South America meant sailing on board a crowded ship for months. Americans wanted to find an easier, faster way to move people and products across the vast expanse of land the United States had claimed for its own.

A Great National Highway
"A Railroad, from some point on the Mississippi, or its tributaries, to some point on the bay of San Francisco, is the best route that can be adopted . . . to open a great national highway from California to the Atlantic coast. . . . It is the duty of this Legislature to encourage the speedy building of a Railroad from the Atlantic to the Pacific, across the territory of the United States."

J. J. Warner, Report on Railroads to the Senate of California, 1851

In the 1860s, before the railroad was built, Pony Express riders delivered mail across the continent. The riders rode 75 to 125 miles (120 to 200 km) and then gave the mail to the next messenger at a station on the route.

A Possible Solution

As far back as the 1830s, people began to talk about building a transcontinental railroad. One of the earliest champions of this idea was New York City businessman Asa Whitney, who tried for years to convince U.S. officials to build the railroad. He and others claimed that the United States would become richer and stronger if people and goods could travel quickly back and forth.

Manifest Destiny

Many white Americans in the 1850s and 1860s believed it was their right and destiny to rule all the land between the Atlantic and Pacific Oceans. They thought their way of life was better than that of Native Americans and that it was their duty to take over the land and impose "civilization" on Indians. The name for this belief was "**Manifest** Destiny," and it was the main reason Americans wanted to build a railroad to reach the West. Missouri Senator Thomas Hart Benton said, "Emigrants would flock upon it as pigeons to their roosts [and carry west] all that civilization affords to enliven the wild domain from the Mississippi to the Pacific."

The woman floating westward in this painting symbolizes Manifest Destiny. She carries a schoolbook and a roll of **telegraph** wire, items representing progress to whites.

The U.S. Army's team of engineers explored the West in the 1850s, looking for a possible route for a railroad. This engraving shows one group's camp in the Rocky Mountains.

Searching for a Route

On March 3, 1853, the U.S. Congress directed Secretary of War Jefferson Davis to map a railroad route from the Mississippi River to the Pacific Ocean. For three years, **topographical** engineers roamed the West. They came up with several possible routes, but they could not find a way over the Sierra Nevada, a mountain range that runs down eastern California and partly into Nevada.

A Report to Congress

"Although the importance of such a work to the prosperity of the nation cannot be doubted, there is reason to suppose that many years will elapse before the resources of the country will be found sufficient for its accomplishment. The natural obstacles to be overcome are the Rocky Mountains and the Sierra Nevada, the deserts between the Missouri and the former chain, and those of the great basin, the flying sands, and the want of timber."

Report of the Superintendent of the Census to the House of Representatives, December 1, 1851

Crazy Judah

In 1854, a young railroad engineer named Theodore Dehone Judah came to Sacramento, California. He became obsessed with discovering a path over the Sierra Nevada. His passion to build a transcontinental railroad was so great that people began calling him "Crazy Judah."

In the fall of 1860, Judah—together with Daniel "Doc" Strong—finally discovered a way over the rugged mountains. The route climbed from California's American and Yuba Rivers to Donner **Pass**. From there, the route angled down to the Truckee River valley and the Nevada desert.

The Big Four

Next, Judah persuaded seven businessmen to start the Central Pacific Railroad. The richest and most powerful of them were known as the "Big Four": Collis Huntington, Mark Hopkins, Charles Crocker, and Leland Stanford, who was appointed as the railroad's president.

The Pacific Railway Act

The U.S. government at last decided to go ahead with the railroad project. On July 1, 1862, President Abraham Lincoln signed the Pacific Railway Act. The new law said two companies would build the railroad. The Central Pacific would lay track east from Sacramento, and the Union Pacific would head west. They would connect their lines at a spot to be decided later. The act also authorized the U.S. government to lend money to the two railroads.

In 1863, Lincoln selected Omaha in Nebraska Territory as the eastern starting point. Construction could now begin.

The railroad station at Omaha was the Transcontinental Railroad's eastern terminal. From there, other railroads would take passengers to cities farther east.

Leland Stanford (1824–1893)

Leland Stanford was born in New York and trained to be a lawyer. After practicing law for just a few years, Stanford headed west in 1852 to join his brothers, who had set up a business selling goods during the Gold Rush. Stanford became a successful merchant in Sacramento and was elected governor of California in 1861. As governor, he gave a lot of state support to the railroad project. In 1885, years after the railroad was completed, Stanford (by this time a U.S. senator) founded Stanford University at Palo Alto, California. It is now one of the nation's top schools.

Chapter Two

Building the Railroad

The Central Pacific

The first rail of the Central Pacific was laid on October 26, 1863. Work was slow on the first stretch between Sacramento and the Sierra Nevada, which lay 128 miles (206 km) to the east. The slow pace was due to a shortage of labor, equipment, and building materials. It took until the end of the following February to lay the first 18 miles (29 km) of track, and the Central Pacific did not reach the mountains of the Sierra Nevada until 1866.

Laying the Railroad

Workers first had to **grade** the roadbed that would support the rail-road. Then they put down a bed of wooden ties, the heavy wooden blocks that connected the rails and held them in place. When the ties were in place, it was time to lay down the parallel lines of iron rails that trains would run on. A group of men would lift an iron rail, carry it to its spot on the track, and drop it into place. This process took only thirty seconds. Workers with sledgehammers would pound ten spikes through each length of rail into the ties beneath it.

These workers are starting to make a tunnel in a sheer rock face. You can see men on the ropes used to reach the rock face and other workers using their picks.

Over the Mountains

Then came the most difficult stretch, through the mountains, where Judah had mapped a twisting, up-and-down route of more than 100 miles (160 km). Workers used **explosives** to blast a path for the railroad out of solid rocks. Dangling in baskets tied to ropes held from above, they drilled holes into the faces of mountains and cliffs. Then they filled the holes with blasting powder and attached **fuses**. After lighting the fuses, the men were pulled up to safety before the powder exploded and tore out huge chunks of rock.

The Anvil Chorus

"It is a grand '**Anvil** Chorus' that the sturdy sledges are playing across the plains. It is in triple time, three strokes to the spike. There are 10 spikes to a rail, 40 rails to a mile, 1,800 miles to San Francisco—21 million times are those sledges to be swung, 21 million times are they to come down with their sharp punctuation before the great work of modern America is complete."

Newspaper report on Union Pacific construction, 1866

In deep snow, railroads sometimes became buried like this stretch in Colorado. Workers had to dig down to the track with shovels.

Dangerous Work

Central Pacific workers carved fifteen tunnels through the Sierra Nevada. The work was dangerous because explosives sometimes ignited too quickly and killed or injured laborers.

Cold and heavy snow also made life difficult and dangerous. During the winter of 1866–1867, forty-four blizzards slowed down the pace of construction to an average of only 8 inches (20 centimeters) of new track a day. The snows grew so deep—40 feet (12 m) in some places—that half the workers were kept busy shoveling snow so construction could continue. Avalanches killed some workers and destroyed supplies and housing.

The Central Pacific did not complete the mountain stretch until April 3, 1868, when the railroad reached Truckee, California, east of the Sierra Nevada. But then the pace picked up. In 1868 alone, the Central Pacific laid 360 miles (580 km) of track as it pushed east to meet the Union Pacific.

A Fierce Competition

As the two railroads got closer to each other, they began to compete to see which could lay track faster. After Union Pacific workers built 8.5 miles (14 km) of track in one day, Central Pacific executive Charles Crocker bet the Union Pacific's Thomas Durant that his railroad could beat that record.

On April 28, 1869, the Central Pacific was only 14 miles (23 km) from the finishing point. More than three thousand Central Pacific laborers began work the minute the sun came up and kept working feverishly until 7:00 P.M. When they were finished, they had set in place 10 miles, 200 feet (16 km) of track, a record that still stands. On that day, workers laid 25,800 wooden ties, 3,520 rails, and drove home tens of thousands of spikes.

In a race to the finish, workers haul away rock, wield pickaxes, and lay ties, while explosives send rocks flying into the air.

Above is a typical busy scene during construction of the Union Pacific across the Plains.

The Union Pacific

It was much easier to lay track on the Union Pacific route. The Transcontinental Railroad runs in an almost straight line between Sacramento and Omaha, and the Union Pacific line was built mostly through flat land on the **Great Plains**. It took a few years for the Union Pacific to get going because the Civil War was raging in the East. When the war ended in 1865, construction went faster.

The workers on the Union Pacific may have had the easier route, but they still had problems. In summer, desert temperatures soared to 110° F (43° C), and water was scarce. Jack Casement, who was in charge of work crews, wrote

Working Song
"Then drill, my Paddies, drill;
Drill, my heroes, drill;
Drill all day,
No sugar in your tay [tea],
Workin' on the U. P. Railway."

Lyrics of a song about Irish Union Pacific workers (known as "Paddies")

his wife about working conditions in central Wyoming: "This is an awful place . . . dust knee-deep. We haul all our water 50 miles (80 km) and we're losing a great many mules, six nice fat ones died in less than an hour today."

Native Americans Fight Back

If the building of the railroad was dangerous and difficult for workers, it was even worse for the Native peoples who lived in its path. The railroad companies were determined to run rails through Indian homelands and to get rid of the buffalo that the Plains Indians depended on. Sioux Chief Red Cloud warned Union Pacific officials: "We do not want you here. You are scaring away the buffalo."

The Plains Indians fought to stop the railroad's invasion of their homeland. They tore up rails, derailed trains by piling logs on tracks, and attacked workers. On August 6, 1867, Cheyenne Chief Turkey Foot and his men derailed a train near Plum Creek, Nebraska, and killed several workers.

Union Pacific chief engineer Grenville Dodge gave the U.S. government a choice: "We've got to clean the Indian out, or give up." So officials sent five thousand U.S. soldiers to protect railroad work crews.

The Union Pacific built many bridges, including a 650-foot (200-m) bridge (above) over Dale Creek in Wyoming.

For the Plains Indians (below), the coming of the railroad meant the loss of their homelands.

After a day of hard labor, Central Pacific and Union Pacific workers needed a place to eat and sleep. A "**perpetual** train" followed them down the track. It had cars used for work, such as blacksmith shops, as well as places to sleep and eat. Sleeping cars were 85 feet (26 m) long and had triple tiers of bunks. Dining cars were big enough to feed 125 men at one time. Every 60 miles (100 km) or so along the route, a temporary town sprang up with a bathhouse and a saloon, where workers could relax. These towns were abandoned as workers laid more track and moved away.

Workers on the Railroad

Railroad workers labored twelve-hour shifts, six days a week. They had titles such as **roustabouts**, **gandy dancers**, and **bridge monkeys**, colorful names that came from the various jobs they performed.

The Central Pacific had trouble recruiting workers until it began hiring the Chinese people who had originally come to California in the 1850s, seeking gold. They proved to be fine, hard workers. The Central Pacific eventually hired more than ten thousand Chinese workers—90 percent of its work force.

Most Union Pacific workers were soldiers who had fought in the Civil War or immigrants from European countries, mainly Ireland. The Union Pacific also employed several hundred African Americans, many of them former slaves.

A group of Central Pacific workers pose for a photograph on a railroad handcar. The car moved along the track when the handle was pumped up and down.

Chapter Three

The Joining of the Rails

A Ceremony

On May 1, 1869, the two railroads ran their lines into Promontory Summit in Utah Territory, the site at which they would be connected. It was a deserted spot 56 miles (90 km) from the town of Ogden.

On May 10, 1869, a ceremony took place to unite the tracks. In the morning, crews from both railroads each laid one last rail. They performed this final task before a crowd of some five hundred onlookers, including railroad officials and workers, soldiers who arrived on a Union Pacific train bound for San Francisco, newspaper reporters, and other people who came to see history being made.

The Golden Spike

The joining ceremony featured a spike made of gold nearly 6 inches (15 cm) long and weighing 14 ounces (400 grams), which was tapped into the final rail to connect the two lines. Telegraph wires had been attached to the spike and the silver hammer used to hit it. When the wires connected with a tap of the hammer, a message would immediately be sent across the country. As the historic message—"DONE!"—was relayed, it set bells ringing in many towns and cities. The spike was removed right away for safekeeping, and it is now displayed at Stanford University.

This photo was taken at the ceremony on May 10, 1869. It shows workers and officials from both railroads clustered around the locomotives that met where the two tracks joined.

Connection Made

At 12:47 P.M., when the speeches finally ended, Leland Stanford swung a silver hammer to drive the last spike into its tie. With the tracks finally connected, the Central Pacific **locomotive** "Jupiter" and the Union Pacific's "Engine Number 119" pulled toward each other.

Driving the Last Spike

"When they came to drive the last spike, Stanford, president of the Central Pacific, took the sledge, and the first time he struck he missed the spike and hit the rail. What a howl went up! Irish, Chinese, Mexicans, and everybody yelled with delight, 'He missed it. Yee!' . . . Then vice president T. C. Durant of the Union Pacific took up the sledge and he missed the spike the first time. Then everybody slapped everybody else again and yelled, 'He missed it too, Yow!'"

Alexander Toponce, eyewitness report

Chapter Four

From Coast to Coast

Riding the Transcontinental Railroad

The Omaha end of the Transcontinental Railroad was linked to other railroads extending to eastern cities. This meant people could get on a train in New York and travel by rail 3,500 miles (5,600 km) to California. Suddenly, a trip that used to take up to six months could be made in seven days!

As soon as the Transcontinental Railroad was finished, passengers and freight began moving back and forth between the two coasts. About 150,000 people made the trip in the first year. Within twelve years, a million people were traveling across the country every year.

The Homestead Act

In 1862, the year he signed the Pacific Railway Act, President Lincoln signed another important new law. This law was the

First-class passengers traveling on the Transcontinental Railroad could eat in the luxurious Pullman's Palace dining cars and sleep in beds in heated sleeping cars.

Homestead Act, which encouraged people to settle in the West and on the Plains by offering them free land. Any family could claim a 160-acre (65-hectare) homestead. They had to settle on it and farm it for five years, and then it was theirs. By the end of the nineteenth century, the law had given 80 million acres (32 million ha) of land to about half a million farmers.

A Boom in the West

The combination of a new railroad and free land drew thousands upon thousands of settlers west of the Mississippi River. The Transcontinental Railroad—and other railroads built in the West soon after—enabled farmers to ship corn, wheat, potatoes, and other products to markets back east. Large cattle ranches appeared in the states of Texas, Arizona, Wyoming, and Colorado because ranchers now had a way to ship their beef to market.

Third-class passengers crowded into cars with hard wooden benches. Many were immigrants from Europe who came to the United States in the 1800s, hoping for land and a new start.

Passengers shoot buffalo from their train. In the 1860s, millions of buffalo roamed the Plains. By 1883, however, fewer than a thousand remained. Killing the buffalo was one method used by white people to eliminate Indians, who hunted the buffalo for food.

Native Americans Suffer

The huge influx of newcomers into their homelands was a disaster for Native Americans. Backed by the U.S. Army, white settlers began taking land away from tribes such as the Sioux, who lived on the Great Plains. When Native Americans fought back against the white invasion, the tribes were gradually defeated and forced to move to **reservations**. After more white settlements sprang up across the Plains, however, even the reservations would not be safe.

Driven from the Face of the Earth

"It is in vain that these poor, ignorant creatures attempt to stay [the railroad's] progress by resisting inch by inch, and foot by foot, its onward march over these lovely plains, where but a few years since they were 'monarchs of all they surveyed.' The locomotive must go forward [over] the hunting grounds of these worse than useless Indian tribes, until they are driven from the face of the Earth."

Silas Seymour, Union Pacific engineer, speaking to Congress, 1868

Broken Treaties

As new settlers demanded more and more land, the U.S. government broke promises that said the reservation land belonged to the Indians forever. Piece by piece, Indian Territory was opened to white settlement. In 1907, the state of Oklahoma was established and Indian Territory, the last haven for Native people, was dissolved.

More Railroads

By 1893, there were more railroads that reached the west coast, their tracks crisscrossing the nation in different areas. These railroads were connected to other lines, and thousands of miles of track formed a network of transportation that covered the entire nation. White settlers followed the railroads, and by 1890, much of the West was occupied by homesteaders, ranchers, and farmers.

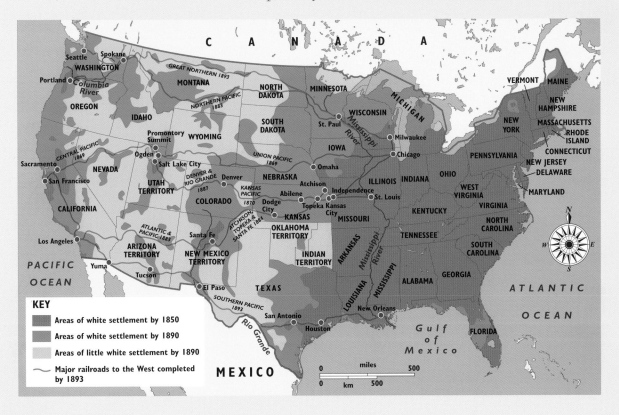

Conclusion

At Promontory Summit, replicas of the two locomotives used in the 1869 ceremony meet on the original Transcontinental Railroad track.

Historic Site

Today, visitors can go to Promontory Summit and see the site of the coupling of the Union Pacific and Central Pacific Railroads. It is part of the Golden Spike National Historic Site, created in 1965 and run by the National Park Service.

Fading into History

The historic site is one of a few places where people can still see steam locomotives puffing their way along a track. In the first part of the twentieth century, steam-powered locomotives gave way to newer, more efficient diesel and electric locomotives. Later in the twentieth century, airplanes, automobiles, and buses began to replace the railroad as the preferred way to travel. Trucks now haul most of the goods once carried by the railroads.

Uniting the Nation

Engraved on the golden spike used in the 1869 ceremony is this inscription: "May God continue the unity of our Country as this Railroad unites the two great Oceans of the world." These words, and the idea of unity, meant a lot because they were written soon after the Civil War. During the war between North and South, the United States had been bitterly divided.

The giant construction project did, indeed, help unite the nation. The railroad also helped make it richer and more powerful, as people had predicted. The new opportunities it offered meant white Americans could now settle all over the continent. Native Americans, however, lost the last of their lands.

A Great Triumph

"The [Transcontinental Railroad] was the first great triumph over time and space. After it came, and after it crossed the continent of North America, nothing could ever again be the same. It brought about the greatest change [in the nation] in the shortest period of time. Only in America . . . was there enough labor or enough energy and imagination [to build it]. 'We are the youngest of the peoples,' proclaimed the *New York Herald*, 'but we are teaching the world how to march forward.'"

Historian Stephen Ambrose

A modern-day train on the Transcontinental Railroad passes the grave of a traveler who died on the Mormon Trail in 1852. Before the railroad, travelers going west faced a long, dangerous journey.

1853 March 3: Congress authorizes U.S. Army to survey possible routes for a transcontinental railroad.

1860 Pony Express begins delivering mail.
Theodore Judah and Daniel Strong discover a route over the Sierra Nevada.

1861 Civil War begins.
June 28: Central Pacific Railroad becomes an official company.
September 4: Leland Stanford is elected governor of California.

1862 May 20: Homestead Act.
July 1: Pacific Railway Act.

1863 January 8: Central Pacific construction begins.
October 26: First rail is laid on Central Pacific Railroad.
November 17: Omaha, Nebraska, is selected as starting point of Union Pacific.
December 1: Union Pacific construction begins.

1865 Civil War ends.
July: Union Pacific construction finally moves out of Omaha.

1866 Central Pacific construction reaches Sierra Nevada.

1868 Central Pacific completes railroad through Sierra Nevada.

1869 April 28: Central Pacific workers build record ten miles (16 km) of track in one day.
May 1: Central Pacific and Union Pacific reach joining point at Promontory Summit, Utah.
May 10: Ceremonial completion of Transcontinental Railroad.

1907 Oklahoma becomes a state and Indian Territory is abolished.

1965 July 30: Congress creates Golden Spike National Historic Site.

Things to Think About and Do

Building the Railroad

Find out more about the methods and equipment used to build the Transcontinental Railroad. Then find out what you can about the methods and equipment available today for building roads. You probably see this equipment being used all the time. Make a list to compare methods and equipment then and now. Think about how long it takes a large machine today to move a few tons of rock and dirt. Then consider how long such work would have taken in the 1860s and what it would have involved.

Homesteader

Imagine your family is heading west to claim a homestead on the Great Plains or in the Rocky Mountains in the 1870s. Describe your journey on the Transcontinental Railroad and what the West was like when you arrived. Find out what you can about life as a settler and write about your family's home, farm, and challenges.

The Coming of the Railroad

Imagine your family is part of a Plains Indian tribe, such as the Sioux, living on the Great Plains in the 1860s. Describe your life before and after the coming of the Transcontinental Railroad. You could write about topics such as where you lived—maybe you had to stop moving from place to place and were made to stay on a reservation. You could describe how you survived, including what you wore and ate when the buffalo were alive and how that changed when they were gone.

Glossary

anvil:	metal block on which other metal is hammered into shape.
bridge monkey:	worker who built train trestles.
explosive:	substance that causes an explosion, usually to destroy or blow apart other substances, such as rock.
fuse:	device, such as a string containing a flammable substance, that can be lit to set off an explosive.
gandy dancer:	worker who laid rails and pounded spikes into rails.
grade:	make a roadbed flat and smooth.
Great Plains:	area of North America between the Mississippi River and Rocky Mountains.
homestead:	property acquired by settlers who staked a claim by living on and farming land rather than buying it.
locomotive:	engine, originally steam-driven, that pulls railroad cars.
manifest:	obviously true and easily recognizable. When white Americans used the phrase "Manifest Destiny," they meant it was obviously their destiny to take over the North American continent.
pass:	low place in a mountain range; and a place where it is possible to pass through a barrier or difficult obstacle.
perpetual:	going on and on.
reservation:	public land set aside for Native American people to live on when they were removed from their homelands.
roustabout:	worker who graded railroad beds.
telegraph:	communication system using coded electrical signals along wires.
topographical:	having to do with the shape of the land.
transcontinental:	crossing a continent.

Further Information

Books

Fraser, Mary Ann. *Ten Mile Day: And the Building of the Transcontinental Railroad*. Holt & Company, 1996.

Gregory, Kristiana. *The Great Railroad Race: The Diary of Libby West* (Dear America). Scholastic, 1999.

Magram, Hannah Strauss. *Railroads of the West* (The American West). Mason Crest, 2002.

Murphy, Jim. *Across America on an Emigrant Train*. Clarion, 2003.

Terry, Michael. *Daily Life in a Plains Indian Village: 1868*. Houghton Mifflin, 1999.

Web Sites

www.cprr.org Great collection of photographs and information on a web site devoted to the building of the Central Pacific Railroad.

www.nps.gov/gosp Information about Golden Spike National Historic Site, maintained by the National Park Service; "In Depth" button leads you to a virtual tour of the park.

www.uprr.com/aboutup/history Good information on the Union Pacific Railroad's web site about the Union Pacific Railroad and how it was built.

Useful Addresses

Golden Spike National Historic Site
P.O. Box 897
Brigham City, UT 84302
Telephone: (435) 471-2209

Index

Page numbers in **bold** indicate pictures.

Benton, Thomas Hart, 8
"Big Four," 10

California, 7, 9, 11, 15, 22
Central Pacific Railroad, **4**, 5, 10, 11,
   12–15, 18, 19, 21, **25**, 26
   see also Transcontinental Railroad
Civil War, 16, 19, 27
Crocker, Charles, 10, 15

Dodge, Grenville, 17
Donner Pass, 10, **10**
Durant, Thomas, 15, 21

East, the, 6, 7

golden spike, 20, **20**, 21, 27
Golden Spike National Historic Site,
   26, **26**
Great Plains, 16, **16**, 23, 24, **24**

Homestead Act, 22–23
Hopkins, Mark, 10
Huntington, Collis, 10

Indian Territory, 25, **25**

Judah, Theodore, 10

Lincoln, Abraham, 11, 22

Manifest Destiny, 8, **8**

Native Americans, 5–6, 8, **8**, 17, **17**, 24,
   25, 27

Omaha, 5, 11, **11**, 16, 22, **25**

Pacific Railway Act, 11, 22
Promontory Summit, 5, 20, 21, **21**, 26, **26**

railroads, 4, 23, 25, **25**, 26
   see also Transcontinental Railroad

Sacramento, 5, 10, 11, 12, **25**
San Francisco, **4**, 13, 20, **25**
settlers and settlement, 5, 6, **8**, 23, **23,**
   24, 25, **25**, 27
Sierra Nevada, **5**, 9, 10, **10**, 12, 14, 23
Stanford, Leland, 10, 11, **11**, 19
Stanford University, 11, 20, 21
Strong, Daniel, 10

telegraph, 8, **8**, 20
Transcontinental Railroad, 4, 5, **17**, **25**,
   26, 27, **27**
   construction of, 5, 12–18, **12**, **13**,
      15, **16**
   hopes and plans for, 6, 7, 8, 9, 10, 11
   impact of, 4–5, 22, 23, 27
   joining of two lines, 5, 20–21, **21**, 26
   links with the East, 4, **11**, 22
   route of, **4**, 5, 9, 10, 16
   traveling on, 22, **22**, 23, **23**
   tunnels, **5**, **13**, 14
transportation, forms of, 4, **6**, 7, **7**, **8**, 26
   see also railroads

Union Pacific Railroad, **4**, 5, 11, 15,
   16–17, **16**, **17**, 19, 20, 21, **25**, 26
   see also Transcontinental Railroad
United States of America, 4, 6, 7, 8, 9,
   11, 17, 19, 25, 27
U.S. Army, 17, 20, 24
   Topographical Engineers, 9, **9**

West, the, 6, 7, 8, 9, 22, 23, 25, **25**
westward travel and travelers, 6, **6**, 7, **7**,
   8, 27
Whitney, Asa, 8
workers, railroad construction, 12, **12**,
   13, **13**, 14, **14**, 15, **15**, 16, **16**, 17,
   18–19, **19**, 20, 21, **21**